AMERICAN CITIZENSHIP

OUR ELECTED LEADERS

by Kate Conley

Content Consultant
Richard Bell
Associate Professor, Department of History

Core Library

abdopublishing.com

Published by Abdo Publishing, a division of ABDO, PO Box 398166, Minneapolis, Minnesota 55439. Copyright © 2017 by Abdo Consulting Group, Inc. International copyrights reserved in all countries. No part of this book may be reproduced in any form without written permission from the publisher. Core Library™ is a trademark and logo of Abdo Publishing.

Printed in the United States of America, North Mankato, Minnesota
032016
092016

THIS BOOK CONTAINS
RECYCLED MATERIALS

Cover Photo: Chuck Kennedy/Executive Office of the President of the United States
Interior Photos: Chuck Kennedy/Executive Office of the President of the United States, 1; World History Archive/Alamy, 4; Nancy Hoyt Belcher/Alamy, 6; iStockphoto, 8, 12, 45; Shutterstock Images, 10; US National Archives and Records Administration, 17; B Christopher/Alamy, 20; J. Scott Applewhite/AP Images, 23; Pete Souza/White House, 24; Brandon Bourdages/ Shutterstock Images, 28; Niday Picture Library/Alamy, 30; Joseph Sohm/Visions of America/ Corbis, 34, 43; Red Line Editorial, 36; Whitney Hayward/Portland Press Herald/Getty Images, 38; Robert Cohen/St. Louis Post-Dispatch/AP Images, 41

Editor: Sharon F. Doorasamy
Series Designer: Laura Polzin

Cataloging-in-Publication Data
Names: Conley, Kate, author.
Title: Our elected leaders / by Kate Conley.
Description: Minneapolis, MN : Abdo Publishing, [2017] | Series: American
    citizenship | Includes bibliographical references and index.
Identifiers: LCCN 2015960490 | ISBN 9781680782431 (lib. bdg.) |
    ISBN 9781680776546 (ebook)
Subjects: LCSH: United States--Politics and government-- Juvenile literature. |
    Political campaigns--United States--Juvenile literature. | Political leadership--
    United States--Juvenile literature.
Classification: DDC 973--dc23
LC record available at http://lccn.loc.gov/2015960490

CONTENTS

CHAPTER ONE

THE DAWN OF A NATION

For eight years, American colonists fought a war against Great Britain. Great Britain ruled the 13 original colonies. Many colonists wanted their independence. So they fought and won. The war became known as the American Revolution (1775–1783). The colonists faced challenges after gaining their independence. The 13 former colonies began operating as separate states. The idea of a

Colonial leaders wrote the Declaration of Independence, a document that spelled out the reasons Americans fought to gain their freedom.

A historical marker in York, Pennsylvania, commemorates the location where the Articles of Confederation were adopted in 1777.

powerful national government was not popular. The people had just fought a war against this type of government.

A group known as the Continental Congress led the states after independence. It used a document called the Articles of Confederation to govern. There were problems though. The Articles created a weak national government. The states held most of the power. By 1787 it appeared the new nation might crumble. The country needed a more powerful national government.

The Constitutional Convention

Delegates from the states gathered in Philadelphia, Pennsylvania, in the summer of 1787. Their goal was to create a plan for a new government. The meeting was called the Constitutional Convention. Delegates argued over how the government should work.

The introduction, or preamble, to the US Constitution begins with the phrase "We the People."

The delegates had to decide how to choose leaders. They also had to decide what powers to give leaders.

The Plan for a New Government

The delegates spent months debating the plan. They made changes and additions. The final document began to take shape. The work was done by September 1787. The result was the US Constitution. By 1790, all 13 states had approved it.

The Constitution spells out how the United States is to be run. The national government is split into three branches. The legislative branch makes the nation's laws. The executive branch makes sure laws are obeyed. The judicial branch interprets the laws. The leaders in the three branches work together. Rules in the Constitution prevent any one branch from being too powerful.

It is possible to change the Constitution. A change is called an amendment. By 2016, there were only 27 amendments. The first ten are called the

The Three Branches of Government

This graphic shows the three branches of government. How does this help you understand how the work of the government is divided? Why might it be useful for these jobs to be separated?

Bill of Rights. Amending the Constitution is difficult.

The process starts with a proposal. This proposal

must pass both houses of Congress. It needs to win

a two-thirds majority in each. Then the proposed amendment goes to the state governments. Three-fourths of the 50 states must approve it.

The delegates crafted the Constitution carefully. They wanted to make sure the nation would last for generations. They wanted US citizens to have a say in government. This voice would take the form of elected leaders.

PERSPECTIVES
Anti-Federalists

Not all Americans agreed with the Constitution. People who disagreed with parts of it were called anti-Federalists. Some states took anti-Federalist views. They felt the Constitution did not do enough to protect individual rights. In response, James Madison and other federalists agreed to write the Bill of Rights. These ten amendments guarantee freedom of speech and religion, among other freedoms. All states eventually agreed to sign the Constitution.

CHAPTER TWO

LAWMAKERS

The US Congress is the legislative branch of the government. Only members of Congress can vote on laws. Congress meets at the US Capitol in Washington, DC.

The House and Senate

Congress is made of two chambers: the House of Representatives and the Senate. Each state has its own representatives and senators. The number of

The US Capitol in Washington, DC, was built in 1800 and later underwent several expansions.

The Three-Fifths Compromise

The issue of slavery was a big topic of debate at the Constitutional Convention. Northerners and Southerners debated whether to count enslaved blacks as part of a state's population. Southerners wanted each enslaved person to be counted as a whole person. This would give areas with slaves more representatives in Congress. Northerners objected to this plan.

The states reached a compromise. Each enslaved person would count as only three-fifths of a person. This way of counting remained in effect until after the Civil War (1861–1865).

representatives each state has is based on its population. Larger states have more representatives. The Senate works differently. Every state has two senators.

There are 435 US representatives. The Constitution has rules about who can become one. A person must be a US citizen for at least seven years. The person must live in the state he or she represents. Also, representatives must be at least 25 years old. They are elected every two years. Representatives hold some special powers. Only representatives can write new tax laws. Only they can remove federal officials from office. And only they can break a tie in a presidential election.

There are 100 US senators. A person must be a citizen for at least nine years to serve as a senator. The person must also live in the state he or she represents. Senators must be at least 30 years old. They are elected every six years. Only senators can approve people appointed to jobs by the president.

Making Laws

The job of senators and representatives is to make

laws. Laws begin as bills. Bills can begin in the Senate or the House of Representatives. If both houses approve a bill, it goes to the president. The president then has several choices. If the president agrees with a bill, he or she can sign it into law. If the president disagrees with it, he or she can veto it. If it is vetoed, it goes back to Congress. Congress can vote on the bill again. If it passes with a two-thirds majority, it becomes law. The president can also choose to neither sign nor veto a bill. If ten days pass and Congress is still in session, the bill becomes law. If ten days pass and Congress has gone out of session, the bill dies. This process is known as a pocket veto.

Other Jobs for Congress

Members of Congress have other jobs, too. Only Congress can declare war against another nation. It has officially declared war 11 times. The most recent time was during World War II (1939–1945). However, Congress does not have to declare war for the military

President Franklin D. Roosevelt signs the declaration of war against Japan on December 8, 1941, after an attack on Pearl Harbor.

to take action. Since World War II, Congress has passed many bills to use troops without declaring war.

Members of Congress create a national budget. They decide how to fund different parts of the government. Major costs include Social Security, health care programs, and the military. Congress can raise taxes to pay for these services. Sometimes the taxes do not provide enough funds. In these cases, Congress can borrow money on behalf of the country.

Members of Congress also help people from their home states. They connect the people they represent with the federal government. For example, a person having trouble collecting Social Security benefits can contact his or her representative. The elected official could look into the problem and try to solve it.

EXPLORE ONLINE

The website at the link below discusses the role of the US House of Representatives. Read about the jobs for the house. They include speaker, minority leader, majority leader, and party whip. Which of these jobs would you be most interested in holding? Why?

Kids in the House
mycorelibrary.com/our-elected-leaders

Sometimes citizens grow frustrated with their elected leaders. They blame the leaders for the nation's problems. President James Garfield reminded citizens that they share responsibility too. Read the following passage from a speech he gave to Congress in 1876:

> Now more than ever before, the people are responsible for the character of their Congress. If that body be ignorant, reckless and corrupt, it is because the people tolerate ignorance, recklessness and corruption. If it be intelligent, brave and pure, it is because the people demand these high qualities to represent them in the national legislature. . . . If the next centennial does not find us a great nation . . . it will be because those who represent the enterprise, the culture, and the morality of the nation do not aid in controlling the political forces.

Source: James A. Garfield. "A Century of Congress." The Atlantic Monthly. UNZ.org, n.d. Web. Accessed February 1, 2016.

What's the Big Idea?

Take a close look at this passage. How does Garfield's speech shift the responsibility of governing the nation? What is the connection between citizens and their elected leaders?

CHAPTER THREE

THE PRESIDENT

The most visible leader in the United States is the president. He or she heads the executive branch of the government. The president must be a US citizen from birth. He or she must have lived in the country for at least 14 years. He or she must be at least 35 years old. These rules are designed to make sure the president is loyal and mature.

George Washington took his oath of office as the first president of the United States on April 30, 1789.

The Electoral College

The Founding Fathers disagreed about how to choose a president. Some delegates wanted Congress to select this leader. Others wanted the citizens to vote directly for the president. They compromised. They created a system called the Electoral College. Citizens vote for the president on Election Day. The result of the vote determines a slate of electors. These electors then actually vote for the president.

Each state has a specific number of electors. This number is equal to the state's total number of senators and representatives. A candidate must win more than half of all electoral votes to become president.

The president lives and works at the White House in Washington, DC. The executive branch he or she leads is in charge of making sure laws are obeyed. This is a large job. More than 4 million people work in the US government's executive branch. Some, such as the president and vice president, are elected. Others are appointed.

Appointing Leaders

Appointing leaders to the executive branch is one of the president's jobs. The Constitution

The Oval Office is where the president meets daily with Cabinet advisors and staff.

President Barack Obama holds a Cabinet meeting at the White House.

requires the president to appoint a group of advisors. They make up the Cabinet. Each advisor leads one of 15 departments. Each department focuses on a particular subject. For example, the Department of Transportation oversees travel by air, sea, and roads.

Working with Congress

The president works closely with Congress. This mainly involves signing or vetoing bills. The Constitution also requires the president to update Congress on the overall well-being of the country. This speech is called the State of the Union address. The president talks about current issues and goals for the next year in the speech.

Other Important Roles

The president also serves as the commander in

PERSPECTIVES
The Kennedy–Nixon Debate

In 1960, John F. Kennedy and Richard Nixon ran for president. They held debates in which they argued about issues. For the first time, these debates were shown on television.

Television viewers noted Kennedy's confidence and energy. Nixon looked sweaty and nervous. People who watched the debate on television felt Kennedy won. Those who listened on the radio believed it was a tie or a slight win for Nixon.

Kennedy won the election that fall. More than half of voters said watching the debates convinced them to vote for Kennedy. Television would forever change presidential elections.

chief of the military. He or she is the top leader of the nation's armed forces. All members of the military must follow the president's orders.

Some of the president's roles are ceremonial. The president may lay a wreath at the grave of a fallen soldier. He or she may welcome foreign leaders or give speeches on holidays. The president represents the American people, their history, and their values at these events.

The original Constitution did not limit the number of terms a president could serve. In 1947 Congress changed the Constitution to set a limit. This was done after Franklin D. Roosevelt had been elected for four terms as president. The states approved the Twenty-Second Amendment in 1951. It says:

> No person shall be elected to the office of the President more than twice, and no person who has held the office of President, or acted as President, for more than two years of a term to which some other person was elected President shall be elected to the office of President more than once . . .

Source: "Two-Term Limit on Presidency." Constitution Center. Constitution Center, n.d. Web. Accessed February 2, 2016.

Changing Minds

This text gives an explanation for why Congress changed the Constitution to limit a president's term. Take the position of Congress. Imagine your best friend has the opposite opinion. Write a short essay trying to change your friend's mind. Make sure you detail your opinion and your reasons for it. Include facts and details that support your reasons.

JUSTICES

The judicial branch of the government is headed by the Supreme Court. The court's job is to decide the meaning of federal laws. It also makes sure laws do not go against the Constitution. The Supreme Court is the highest court in the country. Its decisions are final. They cannot be appealed.

The front of the US Supreme Court Building displays the words "Equal Justice Under Law."

The longest-serving chief justice was Chief Justice John Marshall, who served for 34 years (1801–1835).

A person who serves on the Supreme Court is called a justice. The Supreme Court has nine justices. The leader is called the chief justice. He or she oversees more than 2,000 judges in lower federal courts and a staff of approximately 30,000. He or she administers the oath of office to the president.

The chief justice gives Congress a yearly update on the court. He or she also presides over trials to remove the president from office.

Becoming a Justice

Justices are not elected. They are nominated by the president. The Senate votes to approve the justices. This gives the legislative branch a way to check the president's power.

If approved, justices serve for life. They do not have to worry about being reelected. This

The First Female Justice

Sandra Day O'Connor was born in El Paso, Texas, in 1930. After graduating from law school, she practiced law and later became a state senator and judge. In 1981, President Ronald Reagan appointed O'Connor to the US Supreme Court. The Senate approved her appointment. O'Connor became the first female justice in the court's history. She cast deciding votes on many important cases. Some of the cases dealt with women's rights, personal privacy, and civil liberties. O'Connor served until her retirement in 2006.

PERSPECTIVES

Should Justices Be Elected?

Supreme Court justices are the only nonelected citizens at the top of a branch of government. The Founding Fathers hoped that by avoiding politics, justices could apply the law more fairly.

Some Americans disagree with this idea. They think justices should be elected. They argue that today's justices are making policy through their decisions. For that reason, they should be elected like other policy makers. This idea is popular in some parts of the country. It would require an amendment to the Constitution. This is a difficult and slow process.

protects the justices from the influence of politics. A president has the chance to appoint only a few justices during his or her term. This reduces the influence one president can have on the court.

Citizens do not vote directly for the justices. But a president is likely to appoint justices he or she agrees with. When citizens choose a president, they can have an indirect impact on the court.

The justices of the Supreme Court decide which cases they will hear. Between 8,000 and

10,000 formal requests are filed with the court each year. The court will hear between 75 and 85 of the cases. The justices usually choose cases that affect many people.

FURTHER EVIDENCE

Chapter Four introduced you to the Supreme Court and the justices who serve on it. An important job for the justices is writing opinions on cases. Read the Supreme Court's opinion on *Tinker v. Des Moines*. It is a case about a junior high student and her right to free speech. Do you agree with the court's opinion? Why do you think the justices write different opinions?

The Court's Opinion
mycorelibrary.com/our-elected-leaders

STATE & LOCAL LEADERS

The United States has a federal system of government. This means power is shared between the national and state governments. The Tenth Amendment explains that any powers not listed as federal powers in the Constitution belong to state governments.

The American flag surrounded by state flags

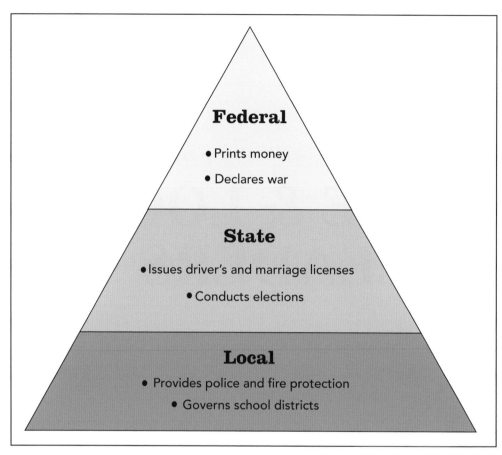

Levels of Government

Each level of government has its own set of duties. This chart shows powers of the national, state, and local governments. How does each level work separately and together to make life better for Americans?

State Governments

Citizens in each state can set up their government however they want. The only condition is that the government is a republic. All state governments are modeled after the national government. They have executive, legislative, and judicial branches. Each state has its own constitution. Nothing in a state constitution can go against the US Constitution.

A governor leads each state's executive branch. He or she is elected by a popular vote. A governor's job is similar to that of the president. The governor makes sure state laws are obeyed. The governor also creates a budget. He or she appears at public events. The governor works closely with the state's legislative branch.

As in the federal government, state legislators cast votes on bills. They also get to know the people in their districts. Lawmakers

From Governor to President

Many national leaders begin their political careers in their state. Their earlier experiences can be a great help to them. In fact, nearly 40 percent of US presidents first served as governors. They include noteworthy leaders such as Thomas Jefferson, Franklin D. Roosevelt, Ronald Reagan, Bill Clinton, and George W. Bush.

A ribbon-cutting ceremony is held to dedicate a new bridge in Saco, Maine, a city of less than 20,000 people.

in rural areas might introduce bills to benefit farmers. Those from cities might introduce bills to improve bus systems. Lawmakers try to act in the best interest of the people they represent.

A high-level court makes up the judicial branch of the state government. It is often called a state supreme court. In most states, judges to the court are either elected by citizens or appointed by the governor or lawmakers. The judges on the court hear cases that involve state laws. If a person loses a case here, he or she may try to take the case to the US Supreme Court.

Influence of Local Government

Elected local leaders often have the greatest influence on a citizen's daily life. They make sure people receive housing permits and ensure that emergency services arrive quickly. These leaders make sure neighborhoods and communities run smoothly.

Local Governments

Below the state level of government are the local levels. They include counties, cities, and towns. Elected leaders at these levels of government include mayors, city councilors, and members of school boards. They manage parks, libraries, and city festivals. They also oversee trash collection and police departments. Judges in municipal courts hear cases at the local level.

At times, all the levels of government must work together. This happens when their interests overlap. For example, if there is a natural disaster, such as a hurricane or earthquake, local, state, and national officials work together. They share information and resources to rescue people and prevent damage.

Voice of the People

Today's United States is vastly different from the country in its early days. But the idea of electing leaders to represent the people has stood the test of time. Today, just as in the past, citizens elect leaders

Government disaster relief workers help a family during winter floods in the Midwest in 2015.

to work toward a better future. They do this across every level of government. Elected leaders continue to serve as the voice of the American people.

FAST FACTS

- The United States is a republic. That means its citizens elect people to represent them.
- The US Constitution outlines how and when national leaders should be elected, who can be elected, and what powers they have once in office.
- Checks and balances in the Constitution prevent leaders in one branch of government from having too much power.
- The Electoral College elects the president. The president's job is to make sure the nation's laws are enforced.
- Citizens elect members of Congress. Their job is to create the laws for the United States.
- All Supreme Court justices are nominated by the president and confirmed by the Senate. The justices interpret the nation's laws.
- Supreme Court justices can decide which cases they hear. Only a small percentage of requested cases are heard.

- Citizens of each state can elect their own government leaders. State governments cannot go against the US Constitution.
- Most state governments are similar to the national government. They have three branches with two legislative houses.
- Local governments often have the greatest impact on a citizen's daily life.

STOP AND THINK

Tell the Tale

Chapter Five mentions that locally elected leaders have a greater influence on the average American than any other level of government. Imagine you have been elected mayor of your city. Write a letter that will appear in the local newspaper, describing three changes you hope to make to benefit all citizens.

Dig Deeper

At the time the Constitution was written, not all Americans had the right to elect their leaders. Women and slaves could not vote. Find an online source that lists the amendments to the Constitution to figure out how and when these voting laws changed. Ask a teacher or librarian to help you research the events taking place in the country that led to changes in the voting laws.

Surprise Me

Chapter One outlines how and why the Constitution was created. What surprised you most about the creation of the US government? Write down three of the most surprising facts. Write a few sentences explaining why each one surprised you.

Say What?

Studying the government and elected leaders can mean learning a lot of new vocabulary. Find five words in this book you've never heard before. Use a dictionary to find out what they mean. Then write the meanings in your own words, and use each word in a new sentence.

GLOSSARY

appeal
a request to bring a legal case from a lower court to a higher court for review

appoint
to choose a person for a position or job

impeach
to charge a public official with wrongdoing or a crime while in office

interpret
to explain the meaning of something

policy
a plan for making decisions in government

Social Security
a government insurance program that provides money for people who are retired or unable to find work

veto
the power of the president to prevent a bill from becoming a law

LEARN MORE

Books

Bausum, Ann. *Our Country's Presidents: All You Need to Know about the Presidents, from George Washington to Barack Obama.* Washington, DC: National Geographic, 2013.

Petersen, Christine. *How the Legislative Branch Works.* Minneapolis, MN: Abdo Publishing, 2015.

Websites

To learn more about American Citizenship, visit **booklinks.abdopublishing.com**. These links are routinely monitored and updated to provide the most current information available.

Visit **mycorelibrary.com** for free additional tools for teachers and students.

INDEX

ABOUT THE AUTHOR

Kate Conley is the author of more than 20 nonfiction books for young readers. She lives in Minnesota with her husband and two children.